T0015638

Amazing
COLOR BY
NUMBERS

ARCTURUS

ARCTURUS

This edition published in 2022 by Arcturus Publishing Limited
26/27 Bickels Yard, 151–153 Bermondsey Street, London SE1 3HA

Copyright © Arcturus Holdings Limited

All rights reserved. No part of this publication may be reproduced,
stored in a retrieval system, or transmitted, in any form or by any means,
electronic, mechanical, photocopying, recording, or otherwise, without
prior written permission in accordance with the provisions of the
Copyright Act 1956 (as amended). Any person or persons who do any
unauthorized act in relation to this publication may be liable to criminal
prosecution and civil claims for damages.

Illustrations: Andres Vaisberg with Diego Vaisberg,
DGPH Design and Visual Arts Studio
Design: Tania Field
Editorial Manager: Joe Harris
Design Manager: Jessica Holliland

ISBN: 978-1-3988-1971-9
CH010338NT
Supplier 29, Date 0622, PI 00001960

Printed in China

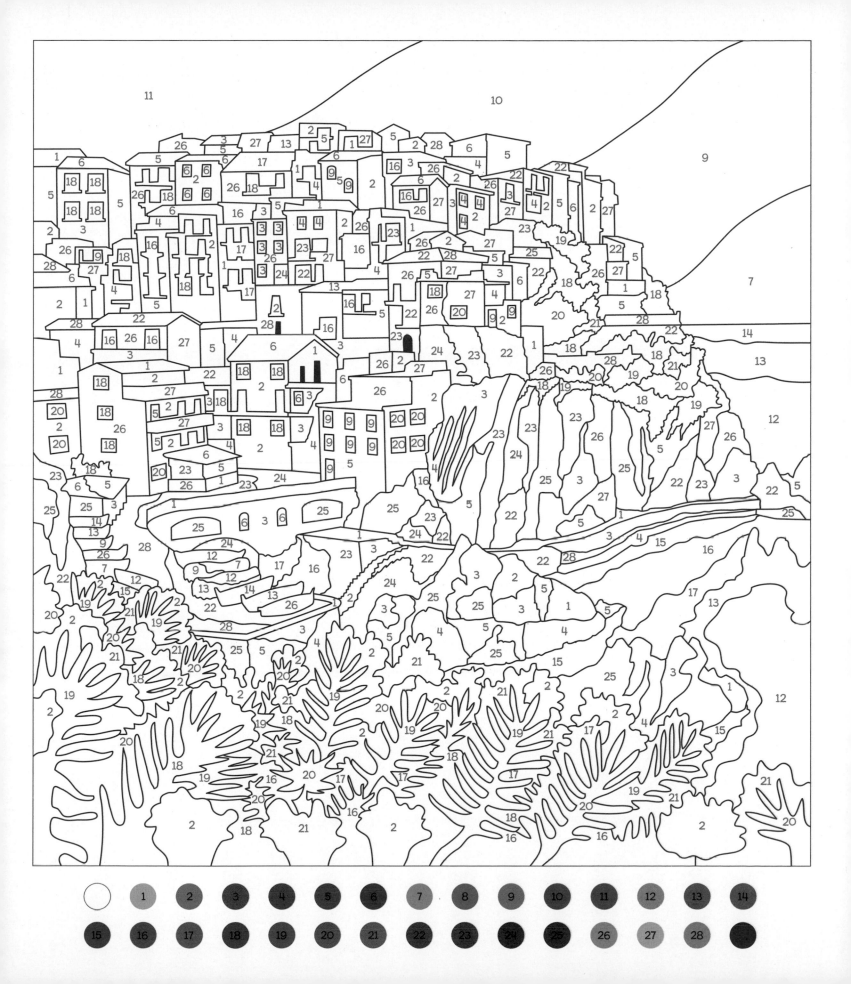

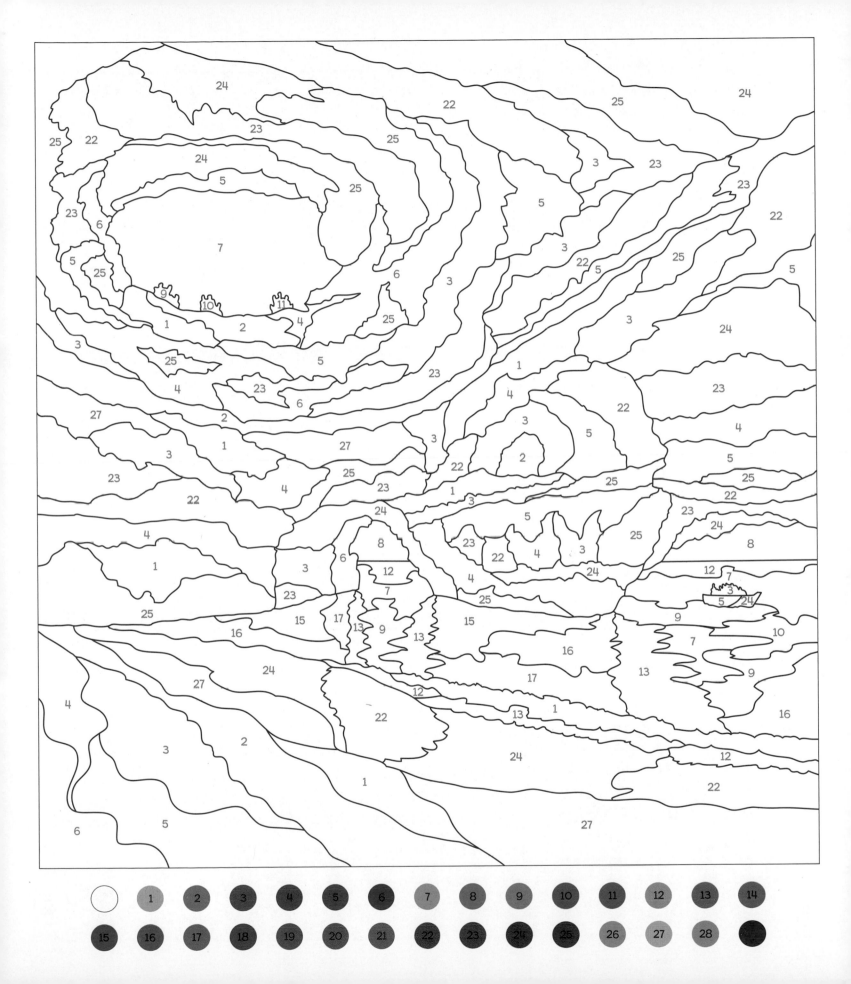